INNOCENCE AND WISDOM
OF MY LITTLE SEEDS

Connie K. Radovanovic

Illustrations by Bruce Tinsley

CR Publishing
Columbus, Indiana 47201

Copyright © 2022 by
Connie K. Radovanovic
All rights reserved

Edited by Kathy Smith
On the front cover is a member of my Little Seeds
Preschool class of 2019/20, during our field trip to a
goat farm. Front cover photography and design by
Kory Callihan, Callihanphotography.com.
On the back cover is the Little Seeds Preschool logo
designed by Lydia Foreman.

First published in 2022
Printed in USA

ISBN: 978-0-578-26769-2
Library of Congress Control Number: 2022910515

Acknowledgments

I wish to thank my dear friends who helped in the selection of the quotes and offered valuable advice: Carol Nelson, Jeannette Smith, Alison Pedersen, Linda White and Kathy Smith. My dear husband was the constant encourager and motivation behind the writing of this book. Without him, the book would have remained just an idea. I also wish to thank all the parents whom I have met and who entrusted me with their children for a brief period to teach, nurture and love. For this opportunity, I am forever grateful.

Dedication

In memory of **Hiroshi Higashino**, a Little Seed who lost his battle with cancer in 2005.

It is also dedicated to these Little Seeds children who have fought a courageous battle with cancer in various forms: **Matthew White, Erin Gordon, Rachel Gore, Burke Tinsley, Kate Madigan, Emma Stamper, Evan Weineke and Justin Spoon.**

Proceeds from the sale of this book will be donated to leading hospitals and research centers working to eradicate cancers in children.

Table of Contents

Innocence and Wisdom of my Little Seeds

Connie K. Radovanovic

History of Little Seeds Preschool

I established Little Seeds Preschool in Columbus, Indiana, in the fall of 1983. Several of my friends and I were seeking an alternative to the preschool programs that were currently offered in Columbus. With treasured memories of my childhood and with a strong desire to be with my children in their early years of development, I assumed the role as founder and director. My dear friends, Linda White and Vicki Washburn, assisted me in forming Little Seeds Preschool, a small, individual-oriented school that presented a prepared environment and respected and preserved the child's rhythm of life. The school's first class had only six 4-year-olds, one of them being my daughter, Mila.

In later years it expanded to include classes for 3-, 4- and 5-year-olds. The classes have remained small in number (8 to 10 children per teacher), and the guiding philosophy has continued to be the beliefs of Maria Montessori, i.e., a prepared environment from which young children, by using their natural curiosity, can absorb knowledge by engaging all five senses. The school was designed to create an environment in which each child could develop at his/her own pace. In the words of Montessori, "We are here to offer to this life the means necessary for its development; having done that we must await this development with respect."

At Little Seeds Preschool, the staff is also dedicated to providing a Christ-centered, caring, loving, individualized, safe and relaxed environment for all children. The staff passionately believes that this environment will help children grow intellectually, socially and spiritually.

Little Seeds provides a balance between academic, social and practical life experiences. Academic areas that receive attention are language, mathematics, science, art, music, movement and spiritual development. Each class is similar to a small family. The child is also given many hands-on experiences — jam making, butter making, woodworking, weaving, sewing, painting, cooking, cleaning, etc. There are field trips to the farm, dairy, greenhouse, historical points of interest, police station, fire station, sawmill, orchard, pumpkin patch, maple syrup site, etc. All these experiences foster children's creativity, make them aware of their abilities and this beautiful world, and help them understand and respect their world and the world of others.

Connie K. Radovanovic

Introduction

What follows are many quotations from children gathered over a 39-year career by myself and my teachers. These quotes are presented as fresh as the day they were uttered — without editing, untouched and raw. The most difficult job was the selection of thousands of quotes contained in memory books.

After going through all the quotes, I have selected ones that I thought were appropriate and made a draft compilation of them. Several dear friends spent hours reading the quotes, selecting the ones most relevant to the title and most humorous.

As I compiled them and thought of these beautiful children who have blessed my life and brought me incredible joy and satisfaction, I recall one quote that continues to guide my passion and devotion to children. One child (when asked to complete a difficult task) said: "Mrs. Radovanovic, you must remember we are just little people."

The book is written for people who wish to laugh along with the preschool teachers who had the pleasure of knowing these precious children. After reading these anecdotes, I hope you will remember the inherent worth of children and the wonder they bring into the world.

Unfortunately, parents often forget many of the funniest moments while kids are little, but maybe these gems will help you remember a humorous story that had been long forgotten.

Children are by nature intuitive, curious and wise, with uncluttered minds and intellectual acuity. They bring to life freshness, joy and wonder missing from the busy world of adults. When we look into a child's eyes, we see eternity.

The chapters are arranged in alphabetical order by the titles and can be read randomly. I sincerely hope that these quotes will bring you a lot of pleasure and warm your heart and your soul.

BODY AWARENESS

Children become quickly aware of and enamored with their bodies and the way they are growing. They notice everything, are uninhibited in commenting on what they observe and often compare their observations to other experiences. During various activities, children draw themselves, families and friends.

1. Dane *(noticing the varicose veins in teacher's legs):* Are those tattoos?

2. Alex *(describing the location of a turkey's red wattle):* See the bump under the teacher's chin? It is just like that.

3. Abby *(to her friends on the tire swing sitting on the tire with knobs):* We have lots of nipples at our house. My dad, my brother and my cat have nipples.

   Children are taking off their sweatshirts.

4. Michelle: I have a turtleneck on.
   Cory: I have on an undershirt under my sweatshirt.
   Alex: I have a belly button under mine.

   Teacher: Eli, why were you absent from school on Friday?

5. My nose was bugging me.

6. Gabe *(having a discussion about what baby worms eat; worms are in a tub on tactile table):* Do worms eat baby food?

   Nick: I don't think so. When I was a baby, I got my food from this machine in my mommy.
   (He raises his shirt to show us his breasts.)
   Hannah: That is not a machine, Nick. Those are boobs!

7. Kooper: Emily, why do you have glitter on your face?
   Emily: This is not glitter. It is sparkles. They are made for your face.
   Kooper: I don't have sparkles on my face.
   Emily: You are a boy. You are not supposed to sparkle.

8. Mason: Teacher, when you swing us in circles, it tickles my privates!

   We trace the children on a large sheet of paper on their special "Me" day and allow them to add any details to the picture. We had just traced Michael, and he had completed his picture by adding eyes, brows, nose and mouth.

9. Kimberly: Michael, you left off your peanut.

10. Eduardo *(commenting on the hole in the knee of another child's pants):* Joshua, your pants are broken. Your knee will get cold.

    Teacher: Children, you must sit on your bottoms during circle time.

11. Devin: My mom says I don't have a bottom.
     Laura *(going over to Devin and looking under his shirt and pants):* Devin, you do have a bottom. I see it.

12. Daniel (*working to make his letters in his journal*):
     The "R" is just like the "P" with one extra leg.

     Teacher: What does your heart do for your body?

13. Nathan: It makes your body beep.

   Teacher: I will kneel down and let you give me a hug that I can enjoy.

14. Mary Claire *(gave the teacher a big hug from behind)*:
   I am looking at your butt. My mom thinks her butt is too big. Do you think my mom's butt is too big?

   Teacher: I haven't noticed. I think your mom is a very pretty lady.

   Mary Claire: I do, too, and I think she is perfect just the way she is.

CHICKENS

Exposure to chickens as a child is an innocent and kid-friendly experience. We often hatched eggs in the classroom. To hold a small fluffy chick and to hear its peep and to feel its heart beat "affords satisfaction to one of the liveliest instincts of the child's mind." (Maria Montessori)

1. David: I like everything at the egg farm except the smell.
   Michael: The saddest thing at the egg farm was that all the workers had to eat just chicken.

   Teacher: *(working on a project to hatch eggs in the classroom):* Why are we putting this light bulb in the box?

2. Tommy: To make them hard-boiled.

3. Luke: If the chicks can hear this noisy classroom, they are probably saying, "Where are we?"

4. Andrew *(getting a baby chick out of the box):* Teacher, do you know what this smells like? Just like McDonald's fries!

   Teacher: We cannot start hatching our eggs in the classroom today. I must first go to the farm and get the eggs.

5. Ian: You can't get them at Kroger because those Kroger eggs don't have a chick inside.

   Laura: That is because the daddy chicken has not done something special to the egg. I don't know what he has to do, but he has to do something.

6. Emily *(looking at the book about the life cycle of chicks):* That rooster is something like my dad. He has a special head, and my dad has one, too, with no hair.

7. Abby: The chicks are coming! The chicks are coming! They're coming faster and faster *(referring to the hatching date on the calendar).*

8. Kathryn: *(describing the chick's vertical posture after a drink):* After every drink of water, that chick prays.

   Teacher: Katie, take this egg carton to Uncle John for his eggs.

9. Katie: He doesn't have any eggs now. The chickens are hibernating.

10. Zachary *(shelling corn):* Do you know that chickens have rocks in their throats and they don't need us to grind the corn for them because the rocks grind?

11. Michael: How do the chickens turn their eggs brown?

12. Daniel: Teacher, are you speaking chicky talk?

13. Avery *(holding a newly hatched chick):* Little chick, don't be scared. Avery will be gentle with you.

Innocence and Wisdom of my Little Seeds

ETHNICITY

I have had the privilege and honor to teach children of many races and ethnic backgrounds. Columbus has many international companies, including Cummins, Toyota Industrial Equipment Manufacturing, NTN and Faurecia, with offices and plants all over the world. Many of their employees come from China, India, Japan and other countries to work here. Our student body reflected this multinational community. Deep friendships were formed, and sincere acceptance and understanding resulted.

1. Hanae *(a little Japanese girl)*: Teacher, I want these Japanese numbers on the calendar. But I am not going to count in Japanese because I'm English now.

2. Isabella: Lily, your cheeks are rosy.
   Lily: I'm Chinese.
   Emet: I'm American. *(He is actually from Ethiopia.)*

   Teacher: Hanae, will you be the Little Red Hen in our play? *(We were re-enacting the story of the Little Red Hen.)*

3. Hanae: Mrs. Radovanobitch, I don't want to be a hen. I want to be a chicken.
   (No, this is not a typo. My last name was often pronounced that way!)

4. Rebekah: Teacher, I have a question for you. I am half Indian. How did this happen?

5. Jude (*practicing our Christmas music*): Gabe, you need to play these maracas. You probably played them when you were growing up in Mexico.

6. Michael *(listening to the book, "The Keeping Quilt," in which several births take place)*: Mason, where did you come from?
   Mason: I came out of my mom's tummy.
   Michael: I came from Mexico.

   Teacher: What was the name of our dumplings that we made during our Korean unit?

7. Natalie: I know. It's Mountain Dew! (*Actually, it is called mondu.*)

8. Shunki *(speaking Japanese to Ayumu — we assume he is telling her to come and sit by him during snacks.)*
   Ayumu: OK. My daddy says I have to make more friends.

9. Jeffrey *(following Mr. Radovanovic into the woods to transplant a dogwood tree):*
   I don't understand what you are saying. I have never heard anyone talk like you!
   (Mr. Radovanovic has a foreign accent.)

10. Hazel: Gauri, why are your hands brown?
Gauri *(who is Indian)*: I don't know.
Hazel: The tops are brown and the bottoms are pink.

---

11. Jonathan *(while painting his Christmas banner)*:
Look! My finger is Grinch green!
Daniel *(who is Chinese)*: Do you know why Chinese people have black hair? They're sort of like Spanish.

Innocence and Wisdom of my Little Seeds

FAMILY

A child's world is anchored and centered within his/her family, where a child learns about love, selflessness, forgiveness, trust, acceptance, self-discipline. If siblings are present, children learn competition, cooperation, sharing, problem solving. Older siblings often become role models and are highly respected.

The family is our incredible laboratory where we learn about life. On various occasions we talked about events in children's lives, e.g., births of siblings, family gatherings, roles of family members, vacations, etc. According to children, there are no family secrets; news about family happenings, good and bad, should and must be shared.

1. Michael *(to another child by name of Michael N.)*: Do you know Ashley already knows who she is going to marry? We need to decide who we are going to marry. And we have to decide if our wife is going to work. I know that my wife is not going to work.

2. Michael N.: I'm not ready for all of this.

3. Kreigh *(sharing a real chain that he received for Christmas)*: I'm going to use this to pull my mom out of her garden when she gets the tractor stuck.

4. Leif: I'm going to have a baby when I get big like my daddy, and I'm going to let him sleep with me.

Working on a biographical sheet at the table with the teacher.

5. Lily: I am your best student!
   Leif: I don't think so. I think my Uncle Mike was the teacher's best student.

6. Reagan: Teacher, do you ever have a dads' kids' night?

   Teacher: What is that?

   Reagan: It is you just do fun things with Dad and snuggle a lot.

7. Nicole: Teacher, you have to come to my house and hide in mine and Marlee's bedroom. You think Seth is a nice boy, but you will see how mean he is to his sisters.

   Teacher: Tell me about your Thanksgiving.

8. Laurel: We had lots of people for dinner: Aunt Patty, Grandma Switzer, Aunt Brenda, Uncle Roy and our neighbors.
   Teacher: How did your mom get all that cooking done?
   Laurel: By us playing outside and not bothering her.
   Teacher: Is Aunt Patty married?
   Laurel: She had a husband, but he moved away.
   Allie: You mean she is 'diversed?'

9. Molly (*telling a new student*): The reason we have a bottom is to sit on.
Andrew: We have a bottom for pooping.
Joe: And for daddies to spank.

Teacher: Why did your parents go away for the weekend?

10. Jacqueline: They wanted to see if Sarah and me could live by ourselves.

Teacher (*speaking to the children about being out of school because of several snow days*): Matthew, was Benjamin (his brother) ready to go back to school?

11. Matthew: He was glad, but not as happy as my mother.

Teacher: Have you been annoying and bothering your mother?

Matthew: Yes, we have, but also that baby has been jumping a lot. (*Mom is pregnant.*)

12. Anna: Ian, why wasn't your picture in the newspaper? Your dad works there.
Ian: He doesn't work. He is just the boss.

13. Corbin: My dad is quitting his job. He is going to stay home with me every day. Don't you think we are going to have fun?

14. Ali: My mom has a hurt shoulder.
    Aubrey: Has she been jumping on the bed?

    Teacher: Morgan, you have a new haircut!

15. Morgan: I did it myself. Mom was at work. Daddy was sleeping, so I took Mom's scissors and cut my hair.

16. Hanae: I want a dog at my house. My dad likes dogs, too.
    Daniel: Who is the boss at your house?
    Hanae: My mom is, and she says, 'No dogs.'"

17. Rachel: I was born last in my family. When I'm home I feel very little, but when I am with you teacher, I feel big.

    Teacher: What are the rules at home?

18. Hannah: Benjamin and Daddy have rules, but I don't. Benjamin's rules are no sloppy eating, no whining, no wasting toilet paper. Daddy's rule is no walking away when it is dinner time.
    John: Just obey, obey, obey my parents.

19. Katie: I have a new cousin; she is a girl. Now my Aunt Jane Ann has four girls and a boy. The boy is her husband.

20. Weston (*Teacher is telling him he needs to learn to zip his pants*): My dad is learning to zip, and he is getting really good at it.

21. Annie: Alisha is not my sister. My mom and dad are just taking care of her. *(Her parents are taking care of a niece.)*
   Bill: What happened to her mother?
   Annie: She doesn't act like a mommy.
   Bill: Why? It is easy to act like a mommy.
   Annie: I don't think she knows how to act like a mommy.

   Teacher: Where did your parents go on their trip?

22. Daniel: I think to another world.

23. Ashley: We didn't get to come to the family field trip. Lauren and I were all ready, but Mommy and Daddy got lost coming home from Bloomington.

24. Chelsea: My mom is going to have twins, a boy and a girl.
   Luke: You know what that means. It means they will come out on the same day.

25. Michael: We're going to build a new house next summer. It takes lots of money; you know, probably two piggy banks full. I have a rabbit one and another one. When they're full, we'll have enough.

26. A boy: I have a funny story about my mom and dad. When they were 16, my mom put my dad's underwear on her head and ran around a tree.

Teacher has finished reading the book, "Oxcart Man." The man in the story bought items needed and placed them in a kettle, tied the kettle to a stick and placed the stick on his shoulder.

27. Graham: That is what you do when you run away from home — tie your clothes in a bag, put the bag on a stick and run.

   Teacher: Have you tried this?

   Graham: No. I just saw it on a tape.

FOOD

Taste is one of our five senses through which we learn. At our school we have snacks every day so there is often quite a conversation about what is served as well as what they eat at home, about the food at our picnic, what they like, etc. Unhealthy eating habits of parents and siblings are often reported.

1. Dane: I had the best lunch, a Happy Meal from McDonald's.
   Zachary: Did you know that McDonald's food is full of grease?
   Charlotte: And it is full of salt.
   Dane: But it was still good

2. Isabella: Teacher, when are we going to have snack (*on the Christmas tree field trip*)? My breakfast is all gone.

3. Eden: My mom says Dad can't fix anything.
   Amanda: My Uncle Bad can fix everything.
   Eden: That is a funny name.
   Amanda: We call him Uncle Bad because all he gives us is junk food.

4. Cole (*commenting on all the crumbs under the snack table*): Don't ask me to get all that stuff under there. I'm not the trash boy.

5.   Will: Emerson, these are the best muffins ever. I ate six pieces, and my belly is so happy.

6. Rachel (*Having strawberries for her birthday snack*): These strawberries came from Walmart. I have a sad story about Walmart. The geese who had their nests there had to move when they built Walmart.

7. Whitney *(arriving at school and realizing that it is "Me" day)*: For crying out loud (*hitting her head with her hand*), I can't believe it. I am the special person, and I forgot my apples.

8. Mickey *(eating a clementine for the first time)*: This is yummy like pancakes, but it looks like a pumpkin.

    Teacher (*Passing out snacks*): I'm sorry, Logan, I forgot to give you snacks.

9. Logan: How could you forget the coolest boy in town?

    Several children were complaining about having apples twice in one week.

10. Zeb: I went to the doctor yesterday, and he gave me shots and said, "Zeb, eat more apples."

11. Katie *(sharing her veggies for V week):* I brought celery, carrots, and radishes. Noah, you should eat this every day.

12.   Tommy: I ate a lot of marshmallows at your house — first two, then two more, then two more, then two more, then I couldn't count anymore.

Speaking about our favorite fruits

13. Nolan: Mine is apples
    Tyler: Mine is apples too.
    Caleb: Mine is peppers
    Zita: Mine is cake!

14. Megi: I am not going to get chickenpox because I'm a vegetarian.

15. Anna: My daddy killed a hog or I think a pig on Saturday.
    Leah (*in amazement*): Your dad did what?
    Nicholas: We have to kill animals if we want meat.

16. Christopher: You know what my dad thinks? He thinks chocolate makes me ballistic.

17. Mila: Teacher, I am making you sausage and eggs with this play dough. I am the sausage, eggs, dessert girl at my house. My dad is the chocolate boy.

    Teacher: Anna, would you like to try a tiny taste of pickle?

18. Anna: No. I wiggle and wiggle after I eat them. Then I throw up.

19. Theo: I am trying to eat all this un-popped popcorn so I'll get a loose tooth.

20. Denise: Bradley, you should eat the apples with their skin on.

Bradley: I don't like them.
Denise: You are going to get very constipated.
Jenna: What is constipated?
Denise: It is when you grunt and grunt, and the poop won't come out.
Chris: My sister has that disease.

21.   Jackson (*on tuna tasting day*): Is this cat food?

FRIENDS

Making and keeping friends help children move forward to a healthy sense of social well-being and help ease separation anxieties. As they begin to value early friendships, they learn social skills, becoming less self-centered, more generous and more concerned about others. Play is so important in this development and facilitates growth and maturity.

During snack time, we use colorful clothing to become natural things:

1. Miah: Aubrey and Abigail, you are the green grass.
   Michael *(whispering to Abigail)*: I don't think you look like grass. I think you are cute.

2. Micah *(as he gets in the van with his friend's mom)*: I have a substitute mom today. So that makes you, Will, and me brothers.

3. Brianna *(taking Davis' hand during activities)*: When you are in preschool, you love the boys. My mom told me this is what you do.

4. Rylan: Max, here is your name tag. You are near Megan. Take care of her.
   Teacher: Why does someone have to take care of Megan? (long silence)
   Rylan: Well, I guess I can tell you. Max is in love with Megan.
   Megan: I can't believe this is happening *(as she hides her head under her carpet)!*

5. Mackenzie: Jasper, I want you to spend the night with me.
   Jasper: I don't think I can because it is a school night, but I'll ask. Where do you live?
   Mackenzie: I live on Beech Street.
   Jasper: You live on the beach?

6. Jasper: Vivian, if you would let me use your shovel, I would marry you.

 Vivian: I guess that's a good deal!

7. Eduardo (*to Emily sitting next to him on carpet working on activities*): I'm too young to be a daddy, but Emily, you are a woman.

 Teacher: I wonder what's wrong with Samuel. He is not participating in sharing, and he is very quiet. I think his lips are locked.

8. Peri (*fluttering her eyes and smiling*): But I have the key!

9. Sophie: I know what we can do. We can throw Megan out the window.

 Teacher: We can't do that.

 Matthew: We surely can't. She is the love of my life.

10. Ella: I think Cristen has been to the beauty shop. She looks so pretty.

 Teacher: Why are you two boys doing the penny game together?

11. Matthew and Zeb just look at each other; they know they should be working separately.

    Teacher: I am waiting for an answer.

    Zeb: Matthew, it is your turn to answer.

12. Will: Blake, I know you know everything, but you don't have to tell me. I already know some things.

13. Matthew: I didn't watch any TV this morning so my brain wouldn't be like cheese. You know like in the poem you read to us. Can't you tell I'm doing better work?
    Amory: I can definitely see a difference.

14. Terynn: I have six whole dollars, and I want to spent it all at Jessi's lemonade stand, and she only wants me to spend 10 cents. Can you believe that?

15. Patrick *(after seeing his friend's baby pictures on his special day):* We have been friends a long time. We even shared our pacifiers when we were babies.

16. Hadley: You know teacher that the boys are just too wild for me. You know that I am rather antique.

17. Annie and Griffin: Teacher, we don't know what is wrong with Sarah. She doesn't want to play with us today.
    Sarah *(usually a demure, cooperative and social young girl)*: I have had enough of both of them!

18. Jonas: Avery, I knew you when you were a kid at school last year. *(Meaning that she has grown over the past year.)*

19. Natalie: Matthew, why are you so pink? You are pink all over.

    Matthew: I always get pink after I play hard.

20. Jenni *(learning to jump from play structure)*: Amory, you jump first and find out how far it is and let me know.

Innocence and Wisdom of my Little Seeds

GENEROSITY

By nature, children are compassionate and generous. Their belongings they hold loosely, ready to give to a friend, a parent or grandparents in need of tenderness from a child. Their hearts have not been hardened by the pain of the world. When a friend is hurting, a hug or some treasured possession is healing balm.

Child is passing out candy that she has brought for dessert for "D" week

1. Reilly: You can have one of each kind.

   Teacher: That is kind of you, but I really don't need the candy.

   Maddy: You are right. When you are old, you don't need candy anymore.

   Bryce: Maddy, you are just being plain mean to our teacher. She is not old, and she needs a little sugar.

   A dear elderly friend who often visited the school had his ear removed because of cancer.

2. Josh: We need to send Mr. Minnick a big hug because he has a broken ear.

Matthew (dumps out all his treat candy at his birthday party).

Teacher: Are you going to share that with your sisters?

3. Matthew: I can't. They are allergic to sugar. Sophie: Well, that is the first time I have ever heard of someone allergic to sugar.

4. Mackenzie: Teacher, you are back to teach us, and Vivian brought snacks. It is going to be a yummy day!

Our visiting speech therapist comes into class to check Davis' hearing.

5. Davis: I brought a dollar for you. *(He goes to get his bag and money and gives it to the therapist.)* Do you ever go to Mancino's *(local pizza and grinders store)?*

Speech therapist: Yes, I like to go there.

Davis: Do you know I own it? (Actually, his dad owns it.)

6. Emily: I'm so happy the sun is shining *(on a cold January day)*.

Teacher: I am too. I hope my sheets dry on the line.

Emily: If they don't, you can come sleep with me at my house.

7. Carter *(opening his birthday present with a grateful heart)*: Wow! My very own rain gauge. I can measure the rain God sends me.

   Teacher has just read the book, "The Cuddlers." What is cuddling?
8. Joshua: I know what cuddling is. I do that with my mom when she is missing my dad. *(Dad is deployed for the military.)* I let her have my blanket and my bear with his army clothes, and I lay close to her.

Innocence and Wisdom of my Little Seeds

GRANDPARENTS

The best playmates that a child could ever have are his/her grandparents. Grandparents have plenty of time, seldom are hurried, can read the same book over and over, tell interesting stories of their own childhood, and can be spontaneous and silly. They delight in sharing their lives with these precious grandchildren. The joy they bring to grandparents cannot be measured.

1. Joe *(Grandpa Jones came to pick him up)*: Grandpa, do you know what I have in my pocket? I have $5, and I am going to take you out for lunch. Where do you want to go?

2. Michael: My grandma is my sleeping buddy. At Christmas, she got me up every night to go to the bathroom. That is how I stopped wearing Pampers. I always told her, "Grandma, you go first" because she is old.

   On the first day of school, Nick wanders out of the safe space to the columbarium; it is near the entrance to the church.

3. Nick: I want to go see my grandpa. He is there. (His grandfather had recently died, and his ashes were placed in the columbarium.)

4. Noah *(introducing his grandmother):* This is Nana.

Nana: I live in a small town in northern Indiana, near the Ohio border.

Tyler: Zita and I both have grandparents who live in Ohio.

Caleb: My grandparents live far away in South Carolina. My grandpa owns a pontoon boat, and he owns my grandma.

5. Allison (*sharing her VIP book that she illustrated*): This is a picture of GaGa and Grandma dancing with me. GaGa can't dance. When he does, it is crazy dancing. He can't sing either. He just says, "Dun, a dun, a dun."

6. Mckenna: My grandma came to school with me today.

   Teacher: Where does your grandmother live?
   Mckenna: In the zoo.

7. Ian: Graham, how old is your grandma?
   Graham: She is old enough to have wrinkles even when she is not wet.

8. Anna: My grandma came on Sunday for my birthday party. Last night, she took out her teeth, but I don't know what she did with them.

   Teacher: How did your grandparents and friends enjoy the tea?

9. Sawyer: Dia (*grandfather*) loved it. We missed him while we were eating, and he was at the cookie table

stealing cookies. I forgot. He wasn't stealing. He is a preacher. He knows better.

10. Ali: Do you know Grandpa Sully loves diving girls.

Teacher: What are diving girls?
Ali: Those girls at the fair that jump off towers wearing their bathing suits. That is why he goes to the fair.

11. Alyssa *(discussing what foods are good for us)*: My grandma loves watermelon, and she is as sweet as watermelon.

Grandma's car will not start when she came to pick up her grandchild.

Grandma: I'm going to have to call Triple A.

12. James: Do they know us?

Soil and Water Conservation visitor, holding up a toothpick. What is this?

13. Emily: Oh, my grandpa needs those because he always gets food in his teeth.
Denise: ... and sugar bugs!

14. Sara: My grandma and grandpa are coming.

Teacher: Which grandparents?
Sara: The funny grandma!

Teacher: Jed, would your grandmother come to school and show us how to knit?

15. Jed: I think she would come. That is all she does all day, making scarfs, socks, sweaters, blankets and dish cloths. Sometimes she takes a break and goes to the grocery store.

HEAVEN

"Let the little children come to me, and do not hinder them, for the kingdom of heaven belongs to such as these." Matthew 19:14

Unabashedly and without doubts, children speak of heaven. They find solace in speaking about it, particularly if some member of the family, a grandparent or someone close has died. Their understanding of heaven makes it real and lifelike.

1. Eduardo (*making a cross using pegs on geoboards*): Do you know why Jesus died on the cross? So he could go to heaven and open the doors for us.
   Abigail: My mom doesn't know that. I'm going to tell her.

2. Jamie (*after the death of his grandmother*): When I go to heaven, I'm going to take my parachute and my umbrella, too. I may want to come back.
   Teacher, are you going to take a parachute?
   Jamie: You will have to take your parachute so you can come back and check on Little Seeds.

51

3. Mackenzie: Teacher, I don't want you ever to die.

   Teacher: Mackenzie, we all will die someday. I just want to do all I can for Jesus and to live like he taught us so I can go to heaven to live with him.

4. Vivian: Heaven is going to be such a happy, happy place.
   Mason: It is going to have to be a big place for all my friends.
   Mikaela: Don't worry, Mason. It will be big enough for everyone, and it will still be beautiful.

5. Ava: I wish I could send a Valentine to GiGi *(grandma)*, but she's up in heaven now.

6. Caleb *(making his night sky T-shirt)*: I'm going to make all my stars gold. Teacher, did you know that when we get to heaven, the streets are going to be gold? And I am going to have a big house there. You can come over anytime and spend the night with me.

7. John *(at snack after prayer)*: My dad can hear all our prayers. He is up in heaven.
   Jessi: Your dad is up there with Uncle Jim, Grandma Jessi and Chu-Chu, my cat.

8. Jenna: I had my mom make you an angel for Christmas because you are an angel.

Teacher: Oh, Jenna, I am not sure I will ever be an angel. I have a long, long, long way to go.

Denise: You surely do, about 2,000 years.

9. Angela (*sending Thanksgiving cards to grandparents*): I have one (*grandparent*) in heaven. I will just put it in the mailbox and write on it: "To Heaven."

10. Kristen: Sam, do you want to go to heaven with me?
Sam: Not now. Maybe when I'm 100 years old.

11. Patrick (*teacher has pushed a dead bird under a bush*): Don't put him under there. He can't get to heaven there. He needs to be out where he can go straight up.

12. Micah (*after hearing the Lazarus story from the Bible*): I wonder how Jesus raised Lazarus from being dead.
Zoe: Because he has the power. You know he is God. I saw him when I was in heaven when I was a baby.
Micah: I think we were all in heaven with God when we were babies.

13. Reilly: When we get to heaven, we are going to be servants of God.
Maddy: I am going to serve him lemonade.
Thomas: I wonder if he likes ice cream.

Teacher: I am so sorry to hear your grandfather died. He is in heaven now.

14. Elizabeth: Not yet. We haven't had the ... ummm ... you know ... the send-off!

Connie K. Radovanovic

IMAGINATION

For a teacher, nothing is more rewarding than to see a child tap into his/her imagination and give it free range to include all possibilities. In childhood, imagination knows no limits. A child takes one idea, adds another and another. He/she is not bothered in the slightest way that reality has been left behind.

1. Andrew (*peeling a carrot with large bump on it*): I think this carrot bumped its head, just like me.

2. Reese (*shelling corn and rubbing dust off the cob*): This is just like fairy dust. I'm going to sprinkle it all around.

3. Reese (*painting with marbles*): Come on marbles, roll! It is just paint.

4. Vivian (*retelling the creation story*): I wonder if God had a blanket and a pillow on the day he rested?

5. Zachary: Teacher, do you know what the ducks could have done on the ark? They could have just jumped out of the boat and swum on the water.

6. Haley (*on the tire swing with eyes closed*): I'm on my way to Kansas to see Dorothy. My head is spinning, and I've lost my mind.

The afternoon class has found several mysteries at school — ants in January, a wooly worm in February

*and frozen leaves in the flower bed in March. One day
we discussed all that:*

7. Kate: This is just a mystery school. I think we should
change its name.

8. Ellen: Did you know when the rain dries up there is a
rainbow? And at the end of the rainbow, there is a honey
pot. I know because the rainbow ended in my yard, and
I called Winnie the Pooh to eat the honey. But he wasn't
there, so I left a message with a rabbit.

   Acting out the story, "Going on a Bear Hunt."

9. Joe: My mom is going to wonder why I am so furry
tonight when I go to bed. I will tell her that I was the
bear everyone was hunting for.

10. Seth: Sometimes I get my pants stuck in my butt.
Emily: What did he say?

   Teacher: Oh, nothing.

   Jared: I think he said he gets ants in his pants.

11. Caroline (*sharing on V Day*): It is something you eat
to make you healthy.
Erin: Vitamins
Another child: My dad doesn't take vitamins. He just
drinks Metamucil.

   Teacher: What are you doing with this fishing
game?

12. Hannah: I'm fishing.
       Teacher*: But the fish are in your hair?*
    Hannah: I am in the water swimming and fishing, but
          you can't see the water.

13. Reilly: Collin, when you were absent last week, you
       missed all the fun. Our teacher brought in a
       hundred frogs and let them loose in our room.
       She also let us paint our clothes and our hair.

    Joseph *(getting close to Reilly's ear)*: What are you
       saying? You know that didn't happen.

14. Maddy (*trying to get her gingerbread dough pliable*): I could sit on it like a bird to make it warm like the bird sits on her eggs to get them to hatch and to keep the little birds warm.

Teacher: Preston, please don't throw the sand. Sand hurts if it goes in people's eyes.

15. Preston: But not when the sandy guy comes at night, right?

16. Josh *(splitting open an acorn eaten by a worm)*: Nobody is at home.

Dancing with a movement instructor to classical music with scarves.

17. Whitney: We are just like Cinderella, dancing while cleaning the house.

18. Chasney (*on the tire swing*): Swing us to Disney World where the princesses live.
Hannah: Swing us to Haiti where there is no fall or winter.

19. Vivian: There was a monster inside my pumpkin at home, and I didn't know it.
Levi (*disappointed*): My pumpkin had only seeds.

20. Leyton (*while milking the pretend cow)*: Come on, cow, get with the program.

Class listening to Christmas story.

21. Nicole: I went to Bethlehem the other night, and I saw baby Jesus, and he was a baby just like in our basket.

22. Kael *(getting ready to go outside to play)*: Can we go to our beach today?
    (The sand area is an old volleyball court and our teeter-totter is there.)

23. Rylan: *(singing the song, "If All the Raindrops were Gum Drops)*: I couldn't catch them with my mouth because they would have wrappers on them.
    Megan: I would catch them with my hands, remove the wrappers and fill my mouth.
    Benjamin: I would just use a bowl to catch them.

24. Erin *(Erin and Devin are pretending to be a stewardess and steward)*: Devin is the drinker, and I am the peanutter.

25. Lauren *(holding up a cup of grape juice during snack time)*: A toast to a very old wine!

26. Daniel: *(on worm day at snack time)*: I think I'm going to quickly turn into a frog so I can eat all these gummy worms.

27. Jacob *(showing his classmates his "Me" folder)*: This is when I was playing football for Ohio State *(an infant picture with a football)*.

28. Addison *(noticing the scarecrows in the room for the first time)*: Looks like we have visitors today.

29. Brett *(while pretending to eat licks for snack on cowpoke day)*: Teacher, do you hear all those pigs?

    Teacher: No, I don't
    Brett: You do not hear all those pigs eating with their mouths open?

30. Daniel *(upon arriving in the safe space with his stick horse on Cowboy Day):*
    Do you have any hay? My horse is hungry already, and he just got to school.

31. Jimmy *(looking at the fall colors)*: Look! Some of the trees are bald.

32. Adam *(becoming very apprehensive about making snow candles in a dishpan)*: Have the cats been using these?

Connie K. Radovanovic

MONEY MATTERS

Early concepts/attitudes concerning money usually are fueled by parents' conversation on the topic. Children soon relate the need to work to earn money. But money earned by them and given to them is generously dispensed.

> **Teacher**: After helping John complete an art project that allowed him to be finished first and choose an activity, asked, "Aren't you going to give me some credit for helping you?"

1. John: I don't have any credit, but my mom has plenty. I will tell her to give you some.

2. Eric: I have something to tell you, teacher. My dad is going to the bank today and put all our money in the bank because my mom has been shopping, shopping, shopping.

3. Laura: You know my friend, Mrs. Brueggemann? I was going to gymnastics with her, and she was speeding. She had to pay lots of money. Kids don't have to go to jail when grown-ups pay.

4. Anna: My daddy had a poor, poor tooth fairy. She left him only nickels.

5. Kaylee: The tooth fairy gives me credit cards instead of money.

   Teacher: Whitney, did you feed your pony the corn you ground?

6. Whitney: My dad was supposed to, but he had to go to work for money. You know work means money, and we have to have money.

7. Emilee: We haven't been to Disney World yet. We are waiting until we win the lottery.

8. Sam: When I am grown up, I am going to have a lot of pets, a raccoon, a skunk, a cat, a dog and an alligator. Bryce: You are going to have a $1,500 carpet bill.

The old record player is making a worn-out sound.
Teacher: Well, children, I think I'm going to have to scrape up some money to buy a new one.

9. Hannah: If you would get a real job, you'll get money.
Jude: First go to the bank, and they will give you some.
Hannah: You can't go to the bank and get money. You first have to put money in the bank.

10. Caleb: I am folding laundry for my mom now at home. She is paying me a lot of dollars.

11. Bradley: My dad makes lots of money by working.
Denise: What does your dad do?
Bradley: He makes gears, and there is lots of money in gears.

12. Whitney: My mom is so angry. When she is angry, she roars like a lion. She went to the bank, and her cards would not work. She has run out of money.

Innocence and Wisdom of my Little Seeds

NATURAL WORLD

Children are born to explore the natural world, an environment that allows them to tap into their sense of awe and wonder. From the experiences of exploring, they form the building blocks for understanding their natural world. But at the same time, imagination is stimulated, and risk taking is learned; exploration is fun, relaxing and exciting.

1. Christopher: I have big news. It all happened last night. It seemed like the middle of the night, but it was actually 5 a.m. My mom came and got me and Justin up to see a foal being born. My mom was so excited she couldn't sit and watch. She had to help the mare.
   One child: Did the egg come out first?
   Christopher: No, it was not in a shell but in a sac.
   One child: What came out first?
   Christopher: The legs. I have pictures at three hours, five hours and seven hours.

2. Anna (*very excited about going to Myrtle Beach with her family*): Do you know that there is plenty of sand for everybody, so you don't even have to fight over it?

3. Ryan (*while visiting a farm*): Why is the bull's poop green and mine is brown?

4. Cole (*on a hike on People Trail*): Oh, there's a broken tree. It's crying.
   Olivia: Maybe it's a weeping willow.

5. Maddie (*describing the bathroom of the teacher's home for a field trip*): She has flowers in that picture, flowers in that wreath, flowers on the wallpaper and fresh flowers. It just looks like a garden in here.

6. Zachary *(sobbing)*: I don't want to go back to school. I want to stay here (*on the maple syrup field trip*). I didn't have any time for self-discovery.

Teacher: Look at the beautiful trees outside. They have so many flowers!

7. Alan: Look at the tree. It is waving to us. (*Alan giggles along with the other children and watches.*) Oh! Maybe it's just the wind.

Teacher: The seed would not grow very well in winter.

8. Logan: We could cover it with a blanket and keep it warm.

9. Nathan: I have two dogs at my house. My Milo is as big as my teacher's dog.
Ella: I had a cat, but he ran away to live with his girlfriend.

Teacher: I brought two cattails for the science table.

10. Joshua (*giggling*): You cut the tails off your cats?

11. Luke (*eating venison cooked with carrots for Thanksgiving feast*): Do the deer come with carrots in them?

12. Brad (*looking at a toad*): His legs are pretty good stretchers.

13. Jackson: I think we are made out of meat. Are we, teacher?

14. Joshua: We are eating all of Sara's delicious pumpkin muffins. We are eating like pigs.
    Parker: No, we are not pigs. Pigs are made out of bacon.

    Teacher: What is one thing you have learned about pet care?

15. Robert (*very serious*): Never take a bath in the same bath with the dog.

16. Andrew: I know how a hurricane comes. The cold water and the warm water mix together in the ocean, and they turn around and around and make a hurricane.

17. Corbin *(commenting on the frog the teacher brought to school)*: Why don't you bring in a squirrel?

> **Teacher**: I don't think I could catch one.
> Corbin: Yes, you could. All you have to do is act like a nut.
> **Teacher**: How would I do that?
> Corbin: I will show you *(curling himself up in a ball on the rug)*.

18. Andrew *(during a discussion about teacher's horse taken away to be bred)*: Will she come back with a whole family?

19. David: They probably just squeeze those cows again and again.

> **Teacher**: Why do you think they call dogwood trees "dogwood"?

20. Valerie: Maybe because someone thought the flowers felt like puppy fur.

21. Hiroshi *(seeing the shocks of wheat in the Amish fields)*: Look, teacher, Indian tepees.

22. Alex *(watching Brandi's pig, which she has brought in for sharing, walk away from him):* Teacher, he looks like he has a human bottom.

23. Mary Zoe (*on farm field trip*): I found soil (soy) beans.

24. John *(coming in from a rain shower)*: Teacher, I have a dozen spiders in my hair.

    Teacher: I don't see any spiders.
    John: I'm teasing. They are just raindrops, but they tickle like spiders.

25. Brian: I know why God made the night. So the stars could have a chance to shine.
    Kristen: So we could rest.
    Sam: So we could see the big, big moon.

26. A.D.: Teacher, I had a stomachache last night, and it stayed up all night with me.

27. Laura (*giving clues for a sharing item*): It is something that grew out of me and something I lost.
    Benjamin: Is it baby fat?

    Visitor is explaining the process of tapping trees and getting sap from sugar maple trees.

28. Alison: Why don't we call it a sap tree?

29. Ellen *(noticing the outdoor stove and steam lifting from the pots)*: Come on, Annie, let's go see what's cooking.

30. Mary: When bears go to sleep in the winter, they go into a cave without their blankies.

Teacher: Does anyone know what the hole at the top of a whale's head is called?

31. Collin: A belly button.
    Alex: It looks like a shower to me.

32. Jennifer: Teacher, come see how our garden is growing. One plant has turned into a baby heart.
    (The first carrot leaf was the shape of a small heart.)

33. Lindsey: Teacher, aren't you glad it's spring? Colds just live in me all winter.

34. Sam *(shelling corn)*: Look, this ear of corn has lost some of its teeth.

35. Cameron: At my lake lot I saw a wood-knocker banging on a tree.

36. Kathryn *(reading a book about life in the forest)*: I know that the daddy owl in the picture is looking for food. That is what dads are supposed to do.

    Teacher is reading a book about a pig farm.

37. Cameron: Look at all those babies getting their dinner.
    Lily: How do they do that?
    Cameron: That mama pig has lots of bottles on her tummy.

38. Allison: On vacation, we saw three dolphins talking and playing, but I don't know what they were saying.

Jack, Jacob and Joshua are lying under a play horse in the big room.

39. Jacob: We are looking for where he uses the bathroom. Jack: We found the place. It is right here under his tail.

40. Ann *(at dairy farm)*: These stinks are giving me a headache.

41. Brian *(looking into a horse's mouth on a field trip)*: I wonder if the tooth fairy picks up these teeth?

   Teacher: Haley, you have such a nice dog pen and play area for your dog, but I don't see the dog.

42. Haley: We had to give him away. He didn't have an off-and-on button.

43. Christopher: Why are you always bringing in things for us to see?

   Teacher: I want to make you curious.

   Kathryn: I think you are trying to turn us into nature girls!

44. John: Teacher, do you want me to sing a drinking song? Do you know what drunk means? It means you get lazy with whiskey. Do you know what whiskey is? It is a drink full of cholesterol.

Matthew: No, it is full of alcohol.

PARENTS

Parents are the most important people in the world to children. They learn to love, respect and adore them. Parents are a child's first teacher and provide the environment for physical, mental, emotional and spiritual growth. Children soon learn the family dynamics, tuning their ears to parents' conversation and giving their own interpretation as to what they have heard.

1. Preston (*working on an activity using a straight sewing pin*): My dad doesn't let me touch these at home. But it is OK. Dad is at work, and he is not watching us.

2. Kimberly *(her dad is late in picking her up)*: I know he has gone out to lunch and forgotten about this child of his.

3. Will: I drew a picture of my mom today, but when I get home, I have to draw tears.

   Teacher: Why is your mom crying?

   Will: She always cries when my dad is out of town. That is all she does.

   Teacher *(Eli's mom had left home early to deliver his brother)*: Eli, where did your mom go this morning?

4. Eli: I think she went on a trip.
5. Lottie (*upon hearing the story of Jesus feeding the 5,000*): This story is making me hungry.

Sophie: I wonder why they didn't bring their lunch.
Emily: They were probably too excited to be with
Jesus.
Eli: Their moms probably forgot to pack them a
lunch. My mom forgets to feed me sometimes,
and I have to go hungry.

Teacher: Hazel, I enjoyed having your dad so
much on our Easter trip.

6. Hazel: He is a very fine man to have around.

7. Claire: Teacher, do you wish my dad was still your
student?

Teacher: I would love that!

8. Claire: I saw the man who told my dad when to grab my
mom and kiss her at the wedding.
*(She had seen the pastor who married her
parents at our church.)*

9. Christie: Do you know what happened at our house? My
dad fell through the ceiling trying to get our
Christmas decorations from the attic and had
blood on his pants.
Ellie (*retelling the above story to her mom, assuming
Christie's dad died*): Christie got a new dad.
Mom: What happened to her dad?
Ellie: He fell through the ceiling.

10. Sarah: Teacher, are you having a bad day? When my mom has a bad day, she just makes lists and lists and lists. Sometimes this helps, and sometimes it doesn't.

11. Christie: I'm a little afraid of this play structure. I cannot jump down.
    Jonathan: Come on, Christie, jump. If you break your bones, my dad will fix them.
    (His dad is an orthopedic surgeon.)

    Making a fall collage:

12. Jonathan: What is this?

    Teacher: It is the seed pod of the native grasses that were growing here when the pioneers came.

    Jonathan: How long ago was that?

    Teacher: About 200 years ago.
    Jonathan: That is when my dad and mom married.

    Teacher: *Josh, did you get your hair cut?*

13. Josh: No, my dad did cut it. My sister got bubble gum in my hair, and Dad just took the scissors and cut it out. My mom was sleeping when this happened, and she wasn't happy when she woke up.

Rebecca returned her turkey craft unrepaired.
Teacher: I thought your dad could fix this.

14. Rebecca: He fixes many things, but he can't fix turkeys.

15. Jonathan: When I grow up, I'm going to move far away from my mom and live with a lady, my wife.
Nathan: I'm going to grow up too and live by myself. I'm not going to have a wife and no kids.
Jonathan: Then you will not get any hugs if you don't have a wife.

16. Nick *(fell into the shelf, hurt his ear and scared his teacher)*: Don't worry, teacher. My dad cut a chunk out of my ear one time when he cut my hair and then my ear came back.

17. Maddy *(the day we are weighing and measuring children)*: My mom has a scale in her bathroom. She and my dad get on the scale a lot. They eat too much chocolate. But they brush their teeth at night, but the chocolate goes to their tummies and makes them fat. I can't call them fat. I have to say they are puffy.

Teacher: Eli, do you have a hug for me before you go home?

18. Eli: Just one because I'm saving four for my mom and dad.

19. Ary: I have a bad cough. Last night I went into mom and dad's bed. It's so nice and warm in there. Sometimes I forget that that's not really my bed.

20. Natalie: My dad wants to move across town. My mom doesn't want to move. My dad says, "If we don't move, can I get a Harley?"

21. Matthew: I know a word that rhymes with cat. Fat. That is what my dad is.
Makayla: Matthew, that is not nice.
Matthew: But that is what he is.

> *One day in early January we had a rainbow after a bad thunderstorm.*
> **Teacher**: Class, did you see the rainbow after school on Monday?

22. Kristin: My mom and I did. She almost wrecked the car. She pulled off the road to take a picture.

23. Katelynn: My mom left yesterday for Iraq. My dad took her to the airport. It is not a trip for kids. I did not get to go.

24. Reilly: My mom dusted for the first time in four years, and she found my rings.

25. Thomas: Teacher, you know when my mom read that award you sent home, she cried. I don't know why she cried.

Teacher: after reading "The Goat in a Rug." What is dye?

26. Joseph: That is what my mom uses on her hair because she wants black hair.

Her mom had brought her to school early on her way to take her dad to the hospital because of a farm accident.

27. Melissa: It is probably just a little paper cut.

(In reality, it was a cut from an auger that required eight stitches.)

28. Matthew: I have something to say. Tom is working on our kitchen, and it is more messed up than when Mom is in it. *(Tom was a construction worker.)*

Teacher: Katie, how does your dad like his new job?

29. Katie: He loves it, but the worst thing about it is he doesn't get to eat lunch with me *(with an extremely sad face)*.

30. Rachel: I can't wait to be a teenager so I can fix my mom's hair.

31. Colin *(commenting on his mom's lateness in picking him up)*: Is my mom walking or what?

32. Alyssa: My mom is always serious when she is cleaning.

33. Brian: Did you get ice cream when you had the
    chickenpox?
  Brian R: Yes, I just went to the store near my house, and
    I did not have to pay for it.
  Megi: If the police had caught you, they may have put
    you in jail.
  Brian R.: I already know all about jail. My dad got put
    in jail several times for speeding.

34. Brian: When my dad gets home from work, we play
everything, baseball, soccer, football, ride our bikes. I get
him so busy, he forgets that it's my bedtime.

35. David: What I want most for my birthday is a snake.
  Jessi: Do you want to scare your mom to death?

36. Emily Rose *(listening to the book, "Now One Foot, Now
Another," about a little boy helping his grandfather learn
to walk after a stroke)*: Once, when my mom was working
on upholstering a chair, she put the wrong side on it, and
she cried. I said, "Mom, don't cry. It is all right to make
mistakes."

37. Robert *(working on a counting activity)*: This is wearing
me out. That's what my mom always says.

> *Learning a song about taking mom breakfast in
> bed for Mother's Day.*

38. Brad: We just call it room service.

39. Kooper: My dad doesn't have to work today.

   Teacher: Is he going to play with you all day?

   Kooper: We are going to play, but first he has to mow the yard.

   Teacher: Children, I want you to make a sign when you get home, "Welcome Home, Dad." Put up a string and use clothespins to hang it.

40. Michael: The sign should read, "Welcome to the Zoo, Dad."

   Teacher *(working on collective nouns)***:** We call a lot of cattle a herd.

41. Gracie: My mom says to my brother when he has a dirty diaper, "Kid, you smell like a herd of goats."

   Teacher *(working on the "Q" sound)***:** Do you ever pretend that you are a queen?

42. Kathryn: No, my mom doesn't have to pretend. She is a queen.

   Teacher: Class, we are going to use a sifter today. Does your mother use a sifter?

43. Emily: I don't think so because Pampered Chef doesn't make them.

44. Anna: My mom had to go and take care of my sick grandma for days. When she got home last night, things were not like she expected. She just got busy going through the house and picking up everything and putting them in a basket, even the dishes. We all had to work to get our things out of the basket, even my dad.

45. Brianna: Amelia, what does your dad look like? Amelia: He looks like a man with no hair. He lost his hair when we were born because he was so scared.

46. Lucas: Did you know the police came to our house last night? My dad locked our dog in the car. We were going on a bike ride and passed the car and saw our dog in there.

47. Cristen: My dad called and said he left his keys in the car. My mom had to take him the keys.

Teacher: Did your mom say, "Silly Daddy, you forgot your keys?"

Cristen: I would rather not say.

48. Hank: My dad is on a diet, but he ate two pieces of my birthday cake anyway.

49. Megan *(looking at Addy's trail mix for snack)*: I think you stole my recipe. My mom made the same thing.

Addy: I don't think my mom would steal.

Teacher: Aren't we thankful that we were all safe at home with our parents last night during the awful storm?

50. Sawyer: I was happy my dad was home. He didn't have a body to work on. (His dad is a mortician.)

51. Matthew: Teacher, do I make you exhausted?

    Teacher: No, you don't.

    Matthew: My mom says I make her exhausted.

52. Tyler: I have turtle and Mickey Mouse underwear, but my mommy has white.
    Emilee: My mom wears pink underwear.
    Julie: My mom has green underwear.
    Another child: My mom has no underwear.

53. Jonathan: Do you know what my mom did when my dad was sleeping? She painted his toenails bright red.

54. Kenna *(singing the Valentine song "Mail Myself to You")*:
If I stuck stamps on my daddy's head, it would hurt when
I pulled them off because he is bald.

Innocence and Wisdom of my Little Seeds

Connie K. Radovanovic

<u>SANTA CLAUS</u>

Most children embrace this age-old character with gusto. And when some question his being, they come to his defense with remarkable stories of his existence and escapades. Their belief in Santa is not easily deterred.

1. Ashley: Teacher, can Santa read?

   Teacher: Surely he can.

   Ashley: I don't think he can. He got so mixed up at our house. He gave the Beauty and Beast doll to my sister, and it was on my list.
   Adam: That Santa didn't leave anything for my mommy in her stocking.

2. Sam: I'll be so happy when it is cold, snowy and Christmas. Santa Claus will come.
   Joseph: There is no Santa Claus. It is just a matter of costumes.

   Teacher *(reading a book)***:** This is a chimney sweep cleaning the chimney for fall and winter.

3. Will: Why doesn't he fall inside?

   Teacher: It is too small for him to fall inside.

   Emerson: But it is not too small for Santa.

4. Marissa: I want a puppy for Christmas. I think Santa is going to bring one for me.

Matthew: He can't bring puppies. They will tear up all the presents.

Anna: Santa could sit puppies on the front seat of the sled with him.

Matthew: Then they would jump out and get lost.

5. Jonathan: There is no such thing as Santa Claus. My dad told me.
   Emilee: I know there is.

6. Logan: Who brings the presents if there is not a Santa?
   Emilee: And when you sit in his lap, you can see he is real. His mustache and beard is not glued on. It grew on him.

   Somebody asked teacher how old is Santa; before she could answer,

7. Joseph said: He is very old. He will be dead soon!

8. Christopher (during a discussion about gifts received for Christmas): Teacher, what did Santa bring you?

   Teacher: A red scarf, red mittens and a red hat.

   Dylan: Santa probably wanted you to look like him.

   Eating Jed's birthday muffins by candlelight.
   Teacher: We have to be very careful with this candle.

9. Quinn: We can't have fire (in the fireplace) or else Santa can't get in.

Innocence and Wisdom of my Little Seeds

SIBLINGS

An older sibling is a small child's first hero. The sibling can do no wrong, but a younger sibling can be a problem. Sometimes rivalry develops for attention and one's own space.

1. Reilly: My sister thinks she is 2, but she is really 1.
   Collin: My sister acts like she is 2, but she is a teenager.

2. Saige (*first one to try our new tire swing*): If I tell my brothers about this, they will say their school is boring, and they will want to come to school with me.

   At the hospital, our nurse explained that all the ill teenagers are placed in a special ward.

3. Michael: I know what those are. We have two of them at our house.

4. Alannah: My mommy is going to have a baby. I'm hoping that it is two babies, a girl and a boy.
   Miriam: That is bad news. You will not be the baby of the family any longer.

5. Rebecca: I have news. Daniel, my brother, likes me. He let me sleep with him last night. It was a very cold night.

Teacher: How is your baby?

6. Jonas: He just learned to giggle.

7. Jude: I have big news — bigger than Christmas. We know the baby that is coming is going to be a boy.

8. Katherine (*turning in her brother's registration material*): I think Jack will do OK here, but he doesn't do a good job at home.

9. Bailee (*Justin is sharing a picture of his sister, Katie, for "K" week*): Do you like her?

   Justin: Yes, I do. She is the best sister in town.

10. Kolten: My little sister runs away from my mom and dad when they want to change her diaper. But she runs to me and hugs me. I actually think she likes me.

11. Violet *(upon receiving her tornado tube, a plastic device that makes a swirl of water in a pop bottle, for her birthday)*: I'm so excited. I'm going to show my brothers something they have never seen.

12. Emily: Can I bring my sisters on the Easter field trip? They love picnics.
    Olivia: I don't want to bring my sister. She is a handful.

13. Josh: I really would like to have a baby brother *(showing a picture of his family on his "me" day)*.

    Heath: I would rather have a dog.

14. John David: Mommy, Daddy, me and two whineys live
    at my house.
    Teacher: Who are the whineys?
    John David: My two brothers.

15. Damon: Teacher, do you know my brother eats out of
    the trash can?

Teacher: What did he find to eat?

Damon: A Pop-Tart.

16. Will *(speaking of sharing his one piece of chocolate gold coin received on St. Patrick's Day)*:
    I am going to give half to Katie *(his sister)* and half to Joseph *(his brother)*, and I will have a tiny piece for me.
    Gabby: I have a too big of family! I am not going to share. It is too small for sharing.

17. Olivia: My sister said to me today, "Be my baby." So I let her put a diaper on me, but don't worry teacher, I changed to my underpants before I came to school.

    A visitor came to school as Abe Lincoln and told the children: "When you go home today, don't fight with your family because a 'house divided against itself cannot stand.'"

18. Andrea: My brother can't stand, and he can't talk either.

19. Jennifer: I learned something new today. You are not supposed to put your elbows on the table. My mother taught me that today.
    Johnathan: My brother should come to your house and learn table manners. He talks with his mouth full, and he can't use a fork or a knife.

SPIRITUALITY

"From the lips of children and infants you have ordained praise." Matthew 21:16

Since children are fresh from God, they are well aware of the spiritual dimension in life. Children's natural curiosity and desire to experience all of life prompt spiritual questions (oftentimes raised in church), e.g., where is God, what is he like, does he see me, is he interested in me, can he communicate with me? In very transparent, honest language, they will reveal their search for answers.

> *Singing the song. "This Train is Bound for Glory."*
> **Teacher**: Where is glory?

1. Maddy: I know it is heaven, and I am going to ask my grandpa to help me get there.

   Re-telling the Easter story to each other using small figures.

2. Eli: What Jesus did for us was a real sacrifice. He loved us so much he died on the cross.
   Will: What is sacrifice?
   Eli: When you do something for someone else, and it hurts.

> **Teacher:** I wonder what you think about Jesus feeding 5,000 people with just five loaves of bread and two fish.

3. Emma (*very seriously*): Where was the tartar sauce?

4. Will (*praying*): Thank you, God, for fishing days with my dad, for skipping stone days, for my fishing bait and my fishing pole.

After reading the book, "Nature's Paintbrush."

5. Anna: Can you believe God made all these beautiful things?

   Leah: He made everything — our activities, our clothes, even our lives.

   Jack: He even made our boxers.

Talking about God creating the world.

6. Nolan: Teacher, were you there when all this happened?

   Teacher sits down with the figures to tell the Bible story.

7. Gabe: Teacher, my heart is ready for the story.

   Teacher: I made a mistake. I'm sorry.

8. Colton: God will give you a second chance, and a fifth chance, and a hundredth chance.

   Singing the song, "Hello, Everybody — God Loves You Today."

9. Emerson: God loves us even when it was raining last night.
   Gabriel: He loves us all the time, even at night.
   Will: I went outside and looked at the sky after the rain. It was awesome!
   Emerson: And God loves us even when we are a little bad.

10. Micah: I hear Jesus talking to me.

    Teacher: What was he saying?

    Micah: He was saying, "Micah, I hope to see you soon."

11. Will (*finding a beautiful brown cecropia moth with white, black and red markings at least 5inches in width*): Look how God surprised me today!

> **Teacher** *(telling the Christmas story)***:** Who was Jesus' mother?

12. Haley: Mary. She was a girl just like me.

> **Teacher**: What was special about her baby?

Leo: He was the son of God.
Davis: He came to save us from our sins.
Joshua: He is the rock and will be with us forever.

> *Teacher is showing the children how to braid. The boys aren't very interested.*
> **Teacher**: Boys, you may have a daughter and want to braid her hair.

13. Joshua: I am going to have all boys, no girls.
    Katie: Joshua, God will decide that. That is not your decision.

14. Cherrie: In my Bible, there is a picture of three gods. The First Commandment says worship one God, so I have figured out that I will worship the one in the middle. He is a little higher than Jesus and the Holy Spirit.

15. Sean (*opening our session with prayer after the death of his uncle*): And God, I am tired of so many people dying, so please stop all this dying.

16. Kristin: I think Adam and Eve rode a horse in the garden.

    Joshua: I don't think so. I have read the whole Bible, and there are no horses in it.

    Someone cut in line at the sink but would not admit it.

17. Joshua: All you have to do is say you are sorry. Then it will be fine.

    Nash: But God gets tired of us saying, "I'm sorry, I'm sorry, I'm sorry." He wants you to mean it and do better.

18. Adam *(praying)*: Dear God, I want to read your Bible every day, but I don't have time today.

19. Delaney: I know what Jesus wants us to do *(after hearing the Mary and Martha story)*. He wants us to pray to him instead of working so much.

    A minister came to class to tell the Easter story. The minister: I wonder what Jesus shouted with his last breath?

20. Adam: He wanted to ask God, "Lord, why are you doing this?"

21. Barrett *(speaking of God as our treasure)*: He is really a very good daddy.

22. Benjamin (*at our gathering and opening prayer*): Dear God, please help my sister to do good on her test. Please help my mom to do a good job cleaning the house today. Help her to get everything sparkling. Amen.

Discussing the creation story:

23. Marlee: I know that story from the Bible.
    Sam: Adam was the first man, and he disobeyed God.
    Will: What is disobeyed?
    Sam: It is when your parents tell you to do something, and you don't do it.

24. Josh: Do you know why we can't see God? Because we're in his hands.

25. Jordan (*discussion about Christmas story*): If there wasn't any rooms or beds for Mary and Joseph, why didn't they bring sleeping bags and sleep on the floor?

26. Allison: Teacher, do you know that Sydney asks me every day, "Allison, how do you run so fast?" I say, "Sydney, I don't know. Ask God." Sydney looked up to the sky and said, "God, why does Allison run so fast?" But God hasn't answered her yet.

27. Caitlin (*listing the things she is thankful to God for*): Christmas, December, Christmas Eve, Jesus and God, my mommy, my friends, all our blessings. (pause) … What are blessings?

28. Matthew *(wondering after hearing the creation story from the Bible)*:
I know why God made us out of clay. So we could hold together.
Joseph: I bet he had the most trouble with the blood. How did he get it to flow all the time?

Teacher: Caleb, give Riley a part of your dough.
(Caleb gives him a piece no larger than a tack.)
Caleb, what does Jesus say about giving?

29. Caleb: He said, "Forgive everyone as I forgive you."

30. Mary Claire: Look at those apples — how shiny! Looks like God just made them.

31. John *(speaking to another student)*: If you are mad and angry all the time, you will go straight to hell. Did you know the devil is in charge there and that it is a place without a happily-ever-after ending?

Children are asking questions about a bombing at Kmart.

32. Jenni: I just don't know why there are so many bad people in the world.
Devin: I think we need another flood.

33. Bradley: I didn't know how to pray until I came to this school. Can I say the prayer all by myself, teacher?
Denise: You have come from a non-prayerful land.

34. Alyssa: God has the best job in the whole world

35. Griffin *(teacher has told the Christmas story and asked why Mary and Joseph rode a donkey)*: I know why they rode a donkey. They didn't have Oldsmobiles.

36. A.D.: Teacher, have you ever seen an angel?

    Teacher: No.

    Jonathan: But I know there are angels.
    A.D.: Then why can't we see them?
    Jonathan: Angels will come to see us when they have important news to tell us.

    Teacher: If you could write a letter to God, what would you tell him?

37. Kevin: I would ask him what he does all day in heaven.
    Jonathan: I would tell him how much I love him.
    Allison: I would thank him for all the birds.
    Patrick: I would tell him how much I like all the things he has made.

    During a bad thunderstorm in September:
38. Michael: Now, it is the time for Noah's true men to get in the ark.

Elizabeth and Nathan working with Nativity set.
Elizabeth has all the creatures and figures in one
area together.

39. Elizabeth: Joseph! Joseph! Where are you?
    Nathan: Over here.
    Elizabeth: Well, come on! Hurry up and get over here!
    We'll leave you here when we go to Egypt. Get
    your camel! Hurry up!
    Nathan *(grumbling under his breath)*: Oh, shut up,
    Mary.

40. Jennice *(selecting the Nativity scene for her first
    activity)*: I just love Jesus. I pray to him every night, but
    my brother, Joshy, he prays too fast. He just says, "God
    bless everybody, Amen."

41. Erin *(commenting on the ghost Caroline pulled from the
    "G" box)*: There is no such thing as a ghost.
    Caroline: Yes, there is; there is the Holy Ghost!

42. Emily *(sharing a picture of her nana)*: She died, but she
    is in heaven eating chocolate cake and dancing.

    Singing the Raffi song, "All I Really Need":

43. Rylan: That singer forgot the most important thing that
    we need. That is God.

    Teacher: You are right, Rylan. Would you like
    to write Raffi a letter to tell him what he forgot?

    Rylan: I can if you help me.

44. Thomas (*working with Jesus activity*): This is God when he was a baby. This is his parents, and these boys brought him presents.

    Teacher: Gracie, I just saw your brother in the other children's program, and he said he is not your brother.

45. Gracie: He doesn't know how to tell the truth yet. He is just learning.

46. Harper: I was supposed to paint Jesus, but I painted a rainbow.
    Claire: Jesus is probably in the rainbow because he made them.

47. Kaitlyn: I feel really happy when I run. I like to run even when it's cold outside. I hope I can run in heaven, with my hair flowing out behind me.

48. Mason (*hearing the Bible story of Jonah*): I don't hear God speak to me.
    Mikaela: I think you have to listen to your heart like my "nene" (grandma) does.

49. Josh (*Gathering at the beginning of our day, he is the line leader. One of his responsibilities is to pray*): I don't think I know the recipe for praying.

50. Emily: Did you hear about the airplane that flew into the building?
    Parker: Those people in the building either went to God or to the hospital.

51. Sydney (*teacher helping Sydney plant bulbs at her home in memory of her infant sister*): When I was in the hospital to see Hannah, the tears would not stop coming.

Teacher is explaining the meaning of St. Patrick, attributing the shamrock to the Father, the Son and the Holy Spirit as mentioned in the scripture or each of the three leaves,

52. Mary Claire: They use that in church when they baptize children. A.D. (*her brother*) used it when he baptized Jimmy's geese.

Innocence and Wisdom of my Little Seeds

TEACHER

A young child usually loves and adores his/her teacher. A bond of friendship develops immediately. The child begins to think that the teacher is extremely smart, can solve all problems and answer all questions. The child will often speak of his/her teacher at home as the authority on various subjects.

> **Teacher** (after a timeout): Nash, do you think I need to send a note home to your mom?

1. Nash: No.
   Addison: Teacher, sometimes you have bad ideas.

> *Teacher has become frustrated in an attempt to finish pig houses for retelling of the story, "The Three Little Pigs."*

2. Shannon: Teacher, you are being quite rambunctious today.

> *In true Montessori fashion, when a new word is introduced to the class, the children repeat it three times.*

> **Teacher:** Anna, I love your pigtails today.

3. Anna: These are not pigtails. They are braids.
   A few days later, teacher makes the same mistake.
   Anna: These are not pigtails. They are braids. Now let's say that word three times, "braids, braids, braids."

4. Violet: We better be working hard. Here comes our teacher.

5. Abby: She may be our teacher, but she is really a little kid inside.

   Teacher: Class, I'm sorry. I have a drippy nose today.

6. Vivian: You have that a lot. It is probably your habitat.

7. Isabella: I don't want to sing these songs, teacher.

   Ainsley: It is just like at home. Sometimes you have to have a boss which is your mom, and the teacher is the boss here at school, and boss tells you what to do.

8. Rachel *(looking at all the pictures of former Little Seeds on the wall)*: Teacher, you must be very, very tired from teaching all those kids.

9. Will *(working on sounds with the teacher)*: It looks like to me that I do not know many. And this is not good. Teacher, what are you going to do about it?

10. Nathan *(trying to do the wooden tangram puzzle)*: Our teacher can do this easy. She has been in preschool a long time.

11. Kayla: Teacher, did you go to Little Seeds when you were a little girl?

    Teacher: No, I didn't go to Little Seeds. I didn't even go to kindergarten.

    Kayla: Did you go to school at all?

    Teacher: Girls, you will have to do a good job on this activity and shade with color pencil the entire shape.

12. Olivia: Teacher, you must remember that we are little people.

13. Josh: Teacher, you should have brought pillows for our heads if you wanted us to lie under this table and paint like Michelangelo did.

    Teacher was using a chair to reach something high.

14. Sawyer: I hope you don't break the chair.

    Teacher is encouraging Graham to finish his snack so he can begin activities.

15. Graham: Did you ever have a day when you just couldn't keep up with the day?

    Teacher: I have those days quite often.

16. Graham: That is the kind of day that I'm having. You understand?

17. Benjamin: Teacher, I'm leaking!

Teacher: You're leaking!?

Benjamin: Yes, I've been running too much. I'm sweaty!

Teacher: Class, we are having some scraps for snacks — a few pretzel pieces, crackers and Goldfish.

18. Caleb: I thought scraps were only for dogs.

19. Devin: Teacher, I drew you on this paper and cut it out for you.
    Alex: That is not our teacher. She doesn't look like a potato!

20. Michael (*to the teacher who wears a scarf in winter*): Why do you always wear that blue towel around your neck?

21. Seth (*teacher had lost her voice*): I know why you lost your voice. You were a grump last night.

22. Brandon (*as the teacher leaned over him to trace his body*): Teacher, did you wash your hair today?

    Teacher: Yes.

    Brandon: Let me smell. It smells clean, but you have gray paint in it.
    A day later:
    Brandon: Did you wash your hair this morning?

    Teacher: Yes.

    Brandon: Well, it looks like you have flour in it today.

    A week later riding with teacher on field trip.
    Brandon: Teacher, you have the dirtiest car in the world. It is almost as dirty as my mom's. I got some buckets and brushes for washing a car, and I am going to come out to your house and wash this car for you. And while I am there, I'm going to try to wash that stuff out of your hair.

23. Peter: Teacher, why do you always wear hose when you wear a dress? They make your legs look and feel funny.

24. Jennifer: Teacher, I want to draw a picture of you for my book. Let me take a good look at you. You have black-and-white hair.

    Denise: But she is not a Dalmatian!

25. Megi: Teacher, you smell new today. Are you wearing something new?

26. LaTasha (*during in-home visit with teacher who is preparing to leave*) to her granny: Am I supposed to love her?

    Teacher *(while class planted soybeans with a block of compressed soil, which was very difficult to break)*: Michael, you must try to break up the soil. You must say, "I think I can, I think I can."

27. Michael: But I can't. Anyways, what you say is not real. It is just in a video about a train.

28. Daniel: This is a state quarter. What state is on this one?

    Teacher: That is Louisiana, my home state where I was born.

    Kyra: Teacher, you aren't even American.

29. Crew: Teacher, you kinda look like a zebra today in that black-and-white shirt.

30. Will: Teacher, you are going to have trouble today. I left my patience at home, and I think Andrew did, too.

Children were doing my poster on teacher's special day

31. Hiroshi: I love you bigger and bigger (*demonstrating with his arms*) every day!

Innocence and Wisdom of my Little Seeds

TRANSPARENCY

"I tell you the truth, unless you change and become like little children, you will never enter the kingdom of heaven." Matthew 18:2

Unlike adults, children, without pretension and un-pharisaical, express feeling openly without inhibitions or fear of embarrassment. They offer comments freely in a loving way without malice or hatred.

> ***Teacher** (on a cold January day)*: Layla, where are your socks? Your feet must be freezing.

1. Layla: No, they are not cold. They are inside my shoes.

   > **Teacher**: Caedmon, why are all the girls chasing you?

2. Caedmon: It is just a mystery.

3. Violet: I really wanted to bring underwear for "U," but Dad said it was a personal item, whatever that means.

4. Kolten: I'm never unhuggable.

   > *After a session when we were shelling corn.*

5. Samuel: We are going to be corn combines today. I see we are shelling corn.

6. Kael: I have corn in my underwear, and it is tickling me.

7. Lindsey: If you look at my ear, you might see a place that looks like a mole, but it really isn't. My mom pulled out a tick that was there. The fun part was when she flushed the tick down the toilet. I bet it was a fun ride like a roller coaster for him.

8. Anika: In the picture of the fish in Alaska, the fish are standing on their tails. (*They are hanging in the market.*)

   Teacher: Addy, carefully and gently place your green hand on the cloth to make your banner.

9. Addy: I'll try, but sometimes you know I act like a bull.

10. Rachel *(looking at the World War II mannequins at the museum)*: That looks like a dead nurse.

11. Isabella *(in bathroom)*: Turn on the light. It is dark in here.
    Class responds: Turn on the light.
    Isabella: How can I? I can't see the light switch.

12. Violet *(having a goodbye hug for everyone at the end of a great morning)*: Kolten is unhuggable *(meaning he was far away from the group).*

13. Daniel (*mixing colors*): Will I get to do this next year?

> **Teacher**: No, Daniel, you will not be in Little Seeds next year.

> Daniel: I think I will. I'm going to high school here.

> **Teacher**: Caroline, you smell so good this morning. What kind of soap did you use?

14. Caroline: I don't remember. My last bath was three weeks ago.

> **Teacher**: You are doing lots of hard work today; you can pretend that you are in kindergarten.

15. Amelia: I don't want to be in kindergarten right now.

16. Evan: I'm so tired today. I want to go home and sleep the rest of my life.
    Anna: You don't want to do that. You would miss Christmas.

> *On Easter field trip, teacher is taking the boys to the bathroom behind the barn.*

17. Trent: I don't see a bathroom.
    Joshua: Just stand here on this hill and aim down.
    Lawrence: Someone has to help me, teacher. I have to take off my coveralls.

18. Matthew (*getting into the van*): Mom, my teacher made me clean myself today, and I did it. Aren't you proud of me? (*He had a big job in the bathroom.*)

19. Alison: My mind told me last night that we can go in the jump house today. Teacher, was my mind right?

    Davis hardly made it to the bathroom and got his pants down.

20. Davis: Teacher, my tee (*pee*) is going crazy, and it is sprinkling all over you.

    Teacher: Class, do not tell your mom about her Mother's Day gift.

21. Megan: I will just tell my dog. He won't tell my mom.

22. Kate: I have nothing to do today. I'm going to play all day.
    (*She didn't have to go to Riley Hospital for cancer treatment.*)

23. Taylor: Teacher, we reuse and recycle everything at this school except diapers.

24. Alyssa: My cousin got married here. We had dinner, and we danced.
    Whitney: You can get married at this school?

One child is speaking some words that we do not use at school; other children want her to repeat herself.

25. Leo: We don't have to know and hear everything.

We are using an imprint of our hands to make turkeys to send as Thanksgiving cards to our grandparents. **Teacher**: Matthew, place the feet, eyes and wattle on your turkey.

26. Matthew: Teacher, this is not a turkey. It is a hand.

Teacher: Collin, I like your rubber boots.

27. Collin: They were made for rain, mud and pigs.

28. Kara: My shirt is called a turtle shell because it's too hard to get your head in.

29. Issac *(He has just received an award for working hard. He comes out of the bathroom ready to go home.)*: I know why I'm having such a good day. I'm wearing my Superman underwear.

30. Kooper: I am wearing really long shorts today.
Emily: They are really capris.
Kooper: Teacher, is that what you call my shorts?

31. Andrew *(after listening to a story about an old lady who swallowed an entire dinner and became a Thanksgiving parade balloon)*: Then she'll poop a lot.

32. Braden: Who are you in love with?
    Jim: No one. Just myself.

33. Barrett *(on Cat Day)*: My mom worked all night sewing this outfit. Please don't pull my tail.

34. Jimmy: Joseph got a shot today, and he cried.
    Jared: Why did someone shoot him?
    Jimmy: They did it to keep him healthy.

35. Devin (*teacher is preparing to play consonant bingo with red markers*):
    I didn't know you could play poker at this school.

36. Katie (*after having an accident in her clothes at school*):
    My mom is going to be so happy when she sees my new panties.

    Teacher: You are to examine this sunflower, and the seeds should stay on the tray.

37. Andrew (*after filling both pockets full of seeds*):
    Teacher, I'm just seeing how many fill my pockets.

    Teacher: Ali, you look pretty today in your black shirt. Is that a paw print on your sweatshirt?

38. Ali: No, it is powder.

    Teacher: I didn't know you wore makeup to school.

    Ali: No, I don't. It is doughnut powder.

    Teacher (urging boys in bathroom to use a small stream of water when washing their hands": We are going to be in a pickle when we run out of water.

39. Jimmy: What is a pickle?

    Teacher: It is a very difficult situation.

    Jimmy (*later during snack time*): We are in a pickle.

    Teacher: How is that?

    Jimmy: There is no water in the drinking fountain.
    (Unit had been disconnected due to building construction.)

40. Mary Claire: My mom didn't send me to kindergarten because she wanted me to be happy, especially in the morning.

41. Robert: I know who is the principal at our school. It is Buddy.
    (Buddy is the custodian.)

42. Chad (*eating a piece of salt dough that he had been told not to eat*): Some just hopped into my mouth. I don't know how it got there. I guess it flew.

    Teacher *(reviewing class on new words learned from unit on Alaska)*: What is the breed of sled dogs called?

43. Denise (*moving to the middle of the circle and doing a cheer*): Go Huskies, Go Huskies, Win! Win! This is what they said at my mom's old school. They were the Huskies.

44. Christopher: There is only one thing wrong with this school. There are too many girls.

45. Libby (*minister visits the class*): He smells good. He is wearing perfume just like my mom's, but I'm sure it was made for a man.

The gentleman who gave us the history of the Quaker cemetery told us that his family had been laid to rest there and that he would be laid to rest there also.

46. Christopher: I don't see any beds.

47. Jonathan (*going home in the car with his parents after open house*): Mom, I feel like all the disobedience has left my body.

48. Mary Claire: I fell down on the way to Bible study; you know on a hill, but not the one Jack and Jill were on, but a different one.

49. Christopher proceeds to take off his pants to share his "T" things.

    Teacher: *What are you doing?*
    Christopher: I am going to share my turtle underwear.

50. Chelsea (*after hearing the book, "The Witch Next Door"*): My mom's broom does not fly. It was just made to sweep sand out of the house.

51. Mary Claire (*on her special day — running back from the bathroom*): Teacher, it may be my special day, but it is not going to be a good day. Mallory just threw up all over the bathroom.

    Teacher: Nathan, I don't hear you singing, and we need to practice these songs for the VIP tea.

52. Nathan: I am singing. You need to go to my doctor and get tubes in your ears.

53. Jenna (*talking about Father's Night activity*): I hope my dad washes his feet before he comes to school. (*On Father's Night activity children paint their fathers' feet.*)

    Teacher: Does anyone remember what special day it is at Little Seeds?

54. Parker: Piney ear (pioneer day).

    Teacher: The pioneers didn't have water that came out of their pipes over the sink like we do.

55. Molly: Why would they buy a house like that?

    Teacher: Please use your walking feet.

56. Will: I can't. These are soccer shoes, and they were made for running.

    Teacher: Dylan, I like your "can do" attitude

57. Christopher: What kind of attitude do I have?

Teacher and class having a discussion about wanting to be older than we are and growing up.

58. Caroline: I don't want to grow up and be a teenager. Then I can't come to Little Seeds.
Allison: I don't want to be a teenager. Then I would be in class with kids who do strange things.

Police officer: What do you do if you break glass at home?

59. Michaela: You better tell the truth.

Teacher: What is patience?

60. Gregory: Waiting without being frustrated.

61. Joshua: Everyone in the class is 5 years old, but our teacher is 12.

62. Emma: Olivia, are those your teenager clothes?

Children are anxious to have snacks.

Teacher: We all have to learn to be patient. There are lots of things for which we have to wait, like starting school, getting your driver's license and getting married.

63. Adam: I'm never getting married.
Michael: Oh, yes you will. You will get used to it.

Teacher: What is a harvest?

64. Burke: It is like at the dinner table. I don't like
tomatoes, but Willa loves them. She harvests
them all.
Gracie: No, that is not a harvest. My grandpa and uncle
gather in the crops with a combine. A combine
separates the grain and cobs. That is a harvest.

Working on making patterns with links.

65. Sam: This seems to have different levels.

Teacher: What kinds of levels?

Sam: Levels of hardness.

66. Alex: What are those hearts with arrows through them
doing on the calendar?
Burke: Those arrows are shot by Cupid when you fall
in love.
Sam: Yikes, yikes, yikes — that must hurt.

67. Sam (*all sitting together in a circle*): There is a (hole)
in this circle. There is a hole in the doughnut,
dear Liza, dear Liza (reference to Gemini song).
Daniel: But there is supposed to be a hole in the
doughnut, Sam.

Quinn is wearing a watch with an alarm. We are sitting in circle time, and the alarm goes off. Quinn jumps up and runs to bathroom.

68. Tyler: Maybe the alarm reminds her to go to the bathroom.
Caleb: Is it a potty watch?

Innocence and Wisdom of my Little Seeds

UNDERSTANDING OF POLITICS

Children are very keen listeners and observers. When they hear an adult conversation, they often repeat it, giving it their own interpretation /understanding of the subject matter, e.g., politics. The more they listen to these conversations, the more opinionated they become, usually taking the political stance of their parents.

Teacher: What do presidents do?

1) Chip: They govern, and they rule.
Anna: They fire people, too.
Denise (*pointing to the presidents*): This is President Washington.
Carl: This is President Lincoln
Denise (pointing to Hillary Clinton): This is the first girl president.
Jonathan: She is the mother of Bush-Clinton.

2) Gabriel: I have big news. Today is Presidents Day. My brother had to go to school as Martin Luther King.

3) Parker: Alex, did you know Al Gore lied?
Alex: No, I did not know that.
Parker: That is why George W. Bush won because he ate the most gummy worms and he told the truth.

Teacher: Burke, you forgot to flush the toilet.

4) Burke: We have Al Gore to blame for this. He wants us to have toilets that use less water. When they use less water, they make more noise. I do not like the noise.

Haley: Who is Al Gore?
Burke: He ran for president against George Governor Bush. Al Gore got the most votes, but George Governor Bush got to be president.

Haley: How do you know so much about the
    presidents?
Burke: My dad tells me these things.

Teacher: We are having squash from Mr.
Bush's farm. You remember our field trip to Mr.
Bush's farm?

5) Evan: We are not talking about the president. It is the
Bush in the pumpkin patch.

Teacher: We celebrate the birthdays of two
presidents, Presidents George Washington and
Abraham Lincoln.

Parker: What about Al Gore?

6) Andrew (*discussing Washington and Lincoln on
Presidents Day and the memorials*): What
about Clinton?

Teacher: He is our president now.
Andrew: But we won't build a building for him,
    because he has been bad.
Erica: What did he do?
Andrew: He lied.

Teacher: Who wears a hat like this (*a stovepipe
hat*)?

8) Ryan: A magic man.
Elizabeth: Frosty the Snowman.
Lauren: President Lincoln.

Collin: President Clinton.

Teacher: Does anyone know who George Washington was?

9) Katie: He was the president of IU.

Connie K. Radovanovic

WONDERFUL LIFE

Each morning is a brand-new day, a day to wonder, to see what it holds, to take it all in, to experience it to the fullest, whereas many adults dread the routine of another day encumbered by work and the demands of life. A parent may fail to understand why a child can slide down the same hill more times than one can count or catch, release and chase a frog until both are exhausted. A child has not done what adults have done nor have they been where adults have been or seen what adults have seen. Life is to be experienced to the fullest. It is a wonder-filled life to a child.

1. Matthew (*telling his mom when she picked him up from the Easter field trip and we were late in returning*): It was the very best day of my life!

2. Sam (*eating chocolate pudding with gummy worms inside*): This is the best dirt I've ever eaten.

3. Trevor (*first time to climb the tulip tree after much contemplation and after being asked if he wanted to do it again*): All in all, kids are to learn things when they are supposed to learn things.

4. Laurel: I am feeling happy today!
   April: I am feeling adorable!

5. Peter: My sister caught a fish, but my mom screamed so loud, she dropped the fish.

6. Sarah: You know why I'm late? There was a mouse in the house. Mommy and I were scared. Hillary's dad had to come and chase him with a broom. We had so much fun that I almost didn't come to school.

7. Brandon: I caught a toad in my backyard. It was brown and gray with bumps and a little smooth and a little rough. I put it in my critter keeper. He ate my cricket. What a learning experience.

Teacher: Jonathan, you can go ahead and return to your activity since we have finished planting.

8. Jonathan: I am just going to stand here and watch my seed grow.

9. Rachel: I was born last in my family. When I'm home I feel very little, but when I am with you teacher, I feel big.

10. Eric (*passing Cummins Inc. building on the way to a field trip*): My dad used to work there, but he changed jobs because he wanted to be closer to Papa John's Pizza.

11. William (*waiting in the safe space before the start of school*): I like the song of the crickets. They just add music to life.

Innocence and Wisdom of my Little Seeds

<u>WORK ETHIC</u>

Children learn about work from their parents or grandparents. If small, age-appropriate jobs are given to a child, he/she accepts it happily and quickly gains self-confidence and skills. Children soon feel that the work cannot be accomplished without them. Children often relate their impressions of how their parents work, the division of labor at home and parental attitudes toward work.

Teacher: Bailee, are you working on an activity?

1. Bailee: I'm working on visiting with my friends.

2. Matthew: I don't want to get old like my dad and have to work all the time and never get to play.
Joe: My dad works, but he still plays a lot.

3. Mackenzie: My dad said he didn't have fun at work yesterday. I don't understand since he has suckers there.

Teacher *(after reading a book about emotions)*: The little girl was sad. She said she had nothing to do. Look at this picture. Do you think she has nothing to do?

4. Maggie: She has something to do — clean her room!

Teacher: Bryce, you should be quietly working with your activity or else you are going to receive the lazy man award.

5. Bryce: I know what it will say: "To Bryce, the last lazy man in the world."

6. Sophie: When we lived in Indianapolis, after my daddy tucked me in, I'd turn on the light and draw.

   Teacher: *Did your dad know this?*

   Sophie: Yes. I call art my job.

   Working at the table with Nick on colored cylinders.

7. Nick: Thank you, teacher, for letting me play with you today. Are you going to play with me the next time?

   We were cleaning each block in our woodworking cart.

8. Kate: Teacher, you are training us to be maids?

   Teacher: Kate, you know the Bible says whatever job God gives you to do, do it well and with joy.

   Sierra: My mom knows that verse really well. She is all the time telling us.

9. Jacob: Teacher, how did you cut all your fingers?

   Teacher: I didn't. My skin cracks when I work hard.

   Jacob: Why don't you stop working?

10. Sarah (*sweeping up the cornmeal*): I do all the work at my house. My sister just talks on the phone all the time to her friends.

11. Laura (*teacher has instructed the students to plant their flowers on the playground before play time*): You sound just like my dad. Work, work, work and then play.

   Teacher: Cristen, I want to see you working!

12. Samantha: But some people don't want to work, teacher.

   Teacher: I enjoy having you so much, Michael, in my class.

13. Michael: I know you do because you like to make kids work, work, work.

14. Bryce (*being the first child to have a birthday at school; teacher gave him work gloves*): I got real work gloves. I love them.

   Maddy: I don't want you to give me gloves for my birthday because I hate to work!

15. Patrick: My dad is the boss, so he doesn't work.

Connie K. Radovanovic

Author

Connie Radovanovic, one of seven children, grew up on a cotton and cattle farm in northeastern Louisiana. Her childhood was carefree, slow and simple, yet one where hard work and responsibility were parental expectations. A favorite pastime was roaming the land — woods, pastures, ponds and creeks among the cattle, chickens, pigs and horses. Life was unscheduled for the children after the work was completed. They were free to play or to walk to a friend's house, at least a mile away.

She received a B.A. in history and English from Louisiana Tech and taught high school in Baton Rouge, Louisiana. After several years of teaching, she returned to graduate school at the University of Alabama, where she earned an M.A. and Ph.D. in European history. Before completion of her doctorate, she taught American history and Western civilization. At IUPUI in Columbus, Indiana, she taught Western civilization, American history and Russian history.

She can be reached at Connie.radovanovic@sbcglobal.net.

Innocence and Wisdom of my Little Seeds

Illustrator

Bruce Tinsley was born in Louisville, Kentucky. While in high school he won a cartoon contest sponsored by Louisville's Voice newspaper chain and began working as an editorial cartoonist at age 16. He graduated from Bellarmine University with a degree in political science. He studied journalism at the University of Missouri in Columbia and attended graduate school at Indiana University School of Journalism with a fellowship he won from Reader's Digest.

In 1994 his conservative comic strip, "Mallard Fillmore," was launched, and it is still published today by King Features Syndicate.

He can be reached at mallardmail@gmail.com.

Innocence and Wisdom of my Little Seeds

Made in the USA
Columbia, SC
06 July 2022

62897612R00080